ANDREW JACKSON

PIVOTAL PRESIDENTS
PROFILES IN LEADERSHIP

ANDREW JACKSON

Edited by Sherman Hollar

Britannica
Educational Publishing
IN ASSOCIATION WITH

ROSEN
EDUCATIONAL SERVICES

Published in 2013 by Britannica Educational Publishing
(a trademark of Encyclopædia Britannica, Inc.) in association with Rosen Educational Services, LLC
29 East 21st Street, New York, NY 10010.

Distributed exclusively by Rosen Educational Services.
For a listing of additional Britannica Educational Publishing titles, call toll free (800) 237-9932.

First Edition

Britannica Educational Publishing
J.E. Luebering: Director, Core Reference Group, Encyclopædia Britannica
Adam Augustyn: Assistant Manager, Encyclopædia Britannica

Anthony L. Green: Editor, Compton's by Britannica
Michael Anderson: Senior Editor, Compton's by Britannica
Andrea R. Field: Senior Editor, Compton's by Britannica
Sherman Hollar: Senior Editor, Compton's by Britannica

Marilyn L. Barton: Senior Coordinator, Production Control
Steven Bosco: Director, Editorial Technologies
Lisa S. Braucher: Senior Producer and Data Editor
Yvette Charboneau: Senior Copy Editor
Kathy Nakamura: Manager, Media Acquisition

Rosen Educational Services
Jeanne Nagle: Senior Editor
Nelson Sá: Art Director
Cindy Reiman: Photography Manager
Brian Garvey: Designer, Cover Design
Introduction by Jeanne Nagle

Library of Congress Cataloging-in-Publication Data

Andrew Jackson/edited by Sherman Hollar. — 1st ed.
    p. cm. — (Pivotal presidents: profiles in leadership)
"In association with Britannica Educational Publishing, Rosen Educational Services."
Includes bibliographical references and index.
ISBN 978-1-61530-941-2 (library binding)
1. Jackson, Andrew, 1767-1845 — Juvenile literature. 2. Presidents — United States — Biography — Juvenile
literature. I. Hollar, Sherman.
E382.A54 2013
973.5'6092 — dc23
[B]
                                                                                2012019291

Manufactured in the United States of America

On the cover, p. 3 (background image): General Jackson *(on horseback)* leads troops against the British
in the Battle of New Orleans. *Library of Congress Prints and Photographs Division*

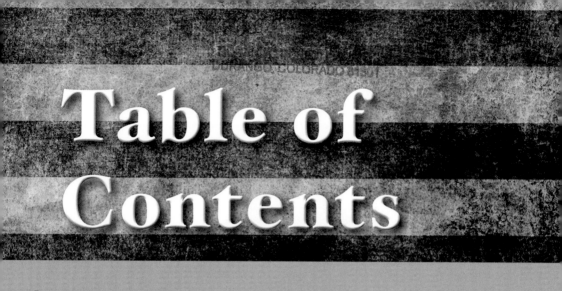

Table of Contents

Portrait of General Andrew Jackson. Library of Congress Prints and Photographs Division

Andrew Jackson's road to the United States presidency was a bumpy one, to say the least. A difficult childhood and limited schooling were among the early hurdles Jackson overcame. Professionally, he faced political infighting, party favoritism, and the stigma of being a nontraditional candidate from Tennessee, which at the time of his election in 1828 was considered a Western state. Through all this Jackson persevered and, as this book details, became a pivotal president in the process.

In many ways, Jackson's childhood unfolded like a tragic work of fiction. He and his two brothers were raised in South Carolina by a single mother, Elizabeth, who was widowed shortly before Andrew's birth in 1767. Elizabeth is believed to have worked as her sister's housekeeper to support her children. The family's lives were further upended by the American Revolutionary War. After the eldest son was killed in battle, his young brothers—Andrew was only 13 at the time—joined the colonial militia. Captured by British forces in 1781, Andrew and his remaining brother, Robert, were taken prisoner. Their mother eventually won their release, but harsh treatment and smallpox contracted while in prison wound up taking Robert's life. Elizabeth died soon after, leaving young Andrew virtually alone in the world.

The experiences of his early life left Jackson understandably edgy and hot-headed. As an adult, he was known for settling even minor disagreements by challenging opponents to a duel. A controlled version of that fighting spirit served him well as the first congressional representative from the new state of Tennessee, in 1796. The next year he was elected to the U.S. Senate, and later was appointed to the Tennessee supreme court.

His combative nature also proved useful when he was asked to take up arms against the British once again, during the War of 1812. An officer in the Tennessee militia, Jackson suppressed a Creek Indian uprising in the South before leading his troops in a victory over the British in the Battle of New Orleans. Jackson also played an important role in the First Seminole War, which hastened the U.S. acquisition of Florida.

Jackson's early life shaped his character and his military service made him a war hero. The latter helped him become president, and the former couldn't help but influence his actions while in office. Jackson made history by being the first president to hail from an area west of the Appalachian Mountains. Furthermore, Jackson did not owe his victory to the support of a well-established political party, which was the traditional means of getting elected. Instead, he won by appealing directly to voters.

During his presidency Jackson faced conflicts with Native American tribes, the threat of secession by South Carolina over tariffs, and soaring inflation. Many would argue that these trouble spots were either created or made worse by Jackson's firm policies. Certainly his administration's refusal to stop the illegal seizure of Cherokee land in Georgia—followed by the forcible removal of the Indians who resisted orders to leave—left a permanent stain on Jackson's record. Yet through his stern leadership he managed to carve out a legacy that also included achievements such as increasing the power of the presidency and greatly advancing the development of popular democracy. As a military leader, politician, and president, Andrew Jackson was a fascinating personality—and certainly a key figure in U.S. history.

CHAPTER 1

Early Life

With a humble political background, Andrew Jackson introduced a new type of democracy in the United States when he became the country's seventh president in 1829. Rather than winning an election through the traditional backing of a strong political party, Jackson triumphed by a direct appeal to a mass of people. He was the first president from the area west of the Appalachians and brought a fresh approach to politics in Washington, D.C.

With a strong will and bold determination, Jackson led the nation with the same rigor that he led his military conquests in the War of 1812 and the First Seminole War, which paved the way for the U.S. annexation of Florida. His fiery disposition commanded the respect

Photo of President Jackson, taken later in life. **Library of Congress Prints and Photographs Division**

of his subordinates, friends, and enemies alike. In the White House, Jackson overcame a domestic crisis with South Carolina over the nullification of federal laws, drove Native American tribes farther west, vetoed the federal bank charter to eliminate banking corruption, and influenced the growth of the Democratic party that stimulated the revival of two-party politics.

CHILDHOOD AND YOUTH

Andrew Jackson was born on March 15, 1767, in Waxhaw, a settlement bordering North and South Carolina. His parents were Andrew Jackson, for whom he was named, and Elizabeth Jackson. The couple lived on a farm in the north of Ireland (now Northern Ireland) near Belfast. Their first two sons, Hugh and Robert, were born in Ireland. The family immigrated to North America in 1765, where the elder Jackson built a home in the forested region of the western Carolinas. The hard pioneer life exhausted him, and he died a few weeks before Andrew's birth, leaving Elizabeth to raise their three sons on her own.

Drawing of the purported birthplace of Andrew Jackson in North Carolina. Hulton Archive/Getty Images

The Question of Jackson's Birthplace

The exact location of Andrew Jackson's birthplace has been debated. Some historians believe he was born at the home of Elizabeth Jackson's sister, Mrs. George McKemy, in the southern part of North Carolina. Others say he was born a few miles farther south across the state border at the home of another of Elizabeth's sisters, Mrs. James Crawford, in South Carolina. In 1824 Andrew Jackson wrote: "I was born in South Carolina, as I have been told, at the plantation whereon James Crawford lived, about one mile from the Carolina Road and of the Waxhaw Creek." Elizabeth and her three sons made their home with the Crawfords, and she worked as housekeeper for her sister to support the boys.

Life in rural Waxhaw was difficult for the fatherless Andrew. He developed into a quick-tempered youth, sensitive to teasing and willing to pick a fight with any of his peers who pestered him. He always defended the smaller boys and taught them how to shoot rifles, fish, race, and wrestle. Elizabeth, who wanted her youngest son to become a Presbyterian minister, provided him with what little schooling existed around their rural frontier home. Starting at age 8, Andrew attended school and learned the basic fundamentals, but he showed little interest in his studies and had no desire to enter the clergy.

The fighting during the American Revolution shifted to the South and interrupted Jackson's early education. He was only 13 years old when the war swept into the Waxhaw region. In May 1780 British raiders won a savage victory over the Waxhaw militia. Andrew and his brother Robert helped their mother tend the wounded in the nearby church. Their elder brother Hugh, a volunteer in a colonial light-horse company, had died after fighting in a battle a few months earlier. Shortly after the Waxhaw slaughter, Andrew and Robert picked up their muskets and joined the colonial militia at the Battle of Hanging Rock, S.C., in August 1780.

The two brothers worked in the Waxhaw militia primarily as mounted orderlies and messengers. The next year Andrew and Robert fought in several backwoods skirmishes against the British. In the spring of 1781, British soldiers captured the boys but failed to break their spirit. When a British officer pointed to his muddied jackboots and commanded Andrew to clean them, the boy

Artist's rendition of a young Andrew Jackson being slashed by a British officer when the former was held prisoner during the American Revolutionary War. **MPI/Archive Photos/Getty Images**

refused. When the officer slashed his saber at the lad's head, Andrew flung up his arm, which partly blocked the blow. He carried scars from these cuts for the rest of his life. Robert also disobeyed the British officer's demand and was cut severely.

The British soldiers took them prisoner and marched the wounded brothers 40 miles

(60 kilometers) over wilderness roads to a prison in Camden, S.C. Their wounds were not treated, and they were provided with no bedding, little clothing, and almost no food or water. Smallpox broke out in the filthy prison, striking both Andrew and Robert. In April 1781 their courageous mother managed to secure their release in exchange for British prisoners at Waxhaw, taking the sick, half-starved boys home. Andrew, fighting delirium, stumbled behind the horses that carried his mother and dying brother.

Robert died a few days later, but Elizabeth's nursing saved Andrew. As soon as he began to recover she made her way 160 miles (260 kilometers) to Charleston, S.C., to help nurse colonial troops held in British prison ships. She soon died of ship fever, but Andrew never learned where she was buried. Throughout his life the memory of her courage and devotion led him to champion and idealize women.

The last of the family, Andrew Jackson was left to make his own way. He spent the next few months with relatives in Waxhaw, where he tried to learn the saddler's trade. At age 16 the restless youth journeyed to Charleston— one of the most elegant U.S. cities of the time.

After living a year in Charleston squandering his inheritance from his Irish grandfather, Jackson decided to become a lawyer.

MARRIAGE AND EARLY CAREER

Jackson moved to Salisbury, N.C., where he studied law for two years before gaining admittance to the North Carolina bar in 1787. Not keen on city life, he wanted to practice law in a more rural setting. The following year he traveled west on the Wilderness Road to Nashville (then part of the western district of North Carolina). There was the true frontier of the United States in 1788—a strong land of mountains, white-water rivers, and tiny stockaded settlements nestled in the wilderness. Standing on the wooded bank of the Cumberland River, Nashville was a village of log cabins. Jackson took lodging at the home of Mrs. John Donelson, widow of Col. John Donelson, one of the founders of Nashville.

Early in 1789 Jackson became a prosecuting attorney in Nashville. He quickly earned a reputation with the local landowners, creditors, and bankers as one of the most proficient lawyers in the territory. These prominent

Portrait of Rachel Jackson, whose first marriage proved problematic years after she wed Andrew. MPI/Archive Photos/Getty Images

citizens became his strongest allies during his turbulent political career.

Living in the Donelson home, Jackson met Rachel Donelson Robards. The daughter of Colonel and Mrs. Donelson, Rachel was living at home, having separated from her husband, Lewis Robards of Kentucky. Andrew and Rachel grew attached to each other during the next few years.

Jackson's marriage to Rachel in 1791 was nullified because the divorce from her first husband was not finalized. The couple remarried on Jan. 17, 1794, but Jackson's neglect in reviewing the legal issues of Rachel's divorce, especially as a lawyer, was exploited by his political opponents in the presidential race of 1828.

Near the end of the 18th century Jackson was fortunate in buying land and holding lands given to him as legal fees. He established a plantation in Nashville and called it Hunter's Hill, where he built a house. While he practiced law, Rachel managed the plantation and developed it into one of the most prosperous in Tennessee.

By 1804, however, Jackson had suffered heavy financial losses. To meet the demands of his own creditors, Jackson sold most of

Log cabins standing on the grounds of the Hermitage in Tennessee. Researchers believe these buildings, which later were used as slave quarters, originally housed Andrew and Rachel Jackson. **MPI/ Archive Photos/Getty Images**

his property, including the Hunter's Hill plantation. The Jacksons moved to a much smaller property 12 miles (19 kilometers) from Nashville and called it the Hermitage. (Hermitage is a term used to describe a secluded retreat or hideaway.) The couple had no children of their own, but in 1809 they adopted a nephew of Rachel's as an infant, naming him Andrew Jackson, Jr. Within a few years they developed the Hermitage into one of the most famous plantations in the country.

An innovative and resourceful farmer, Jackson was one of the first to use a cotton gin, which greatly increased his output of the valuable crop. He raised and sold the finest horses in the region. Under Rachel's direction, their wide fields yielded rich harvests of cotton, corn, and wheat.

Entry into Politics

Jackson won respect for his blunt fairness as a prosecutor and his willingness to challenge

Jackson shooting lawyer Charles Dickinson during a duel that killed Dickinson and wounded Jackson for life. **Library of Congress Prints and Photographs Division**

THE DUEL.

anyone who disputed him to a duel. One such confrontation occurred in 1806 with fellow lawyer Charles Dickinson, and Jackson was shot in the chest before killing Dickinson. The bullet could not be removed because of its proximity to Jackson's heart, and it remained lodged in his body for the rest of his life.

In early 1796 Jackson was a delegate to the Tennessee constitutional convention that was preparing for statehood. When Tennessee was admitted as the 16th state in June 1796, it was entitled to only one representative in Congress. That same year Jackson was elected as the first Tennessee delegate to the United States House of Representatives.

At that time, the nation's capital was in Philadelphia, an old city proud of its culture and refinement. The national government was in the hands of the Eastern aristocracy. Jackson arrived into this staid city in December 1796 as "the man from the West," and Philadelphia had rarely seen anything like his bold spirit.

Jackson at once showed Congress his fiery personality. Although he was not a skilled orator, his fervid speeches portrayed how earnestly he believed in his principles. U.S.

Secretary of State Thomas Jefferson said that Jackson's "violent passions choked his utterance." Jackson firmly believed in Jefferson's democratic ideals of individual freedoms and states' rights as opposed to the Federalist program, which favored a powerful federal government. When Congress proposed a resolution to approve the Federalist administration of President George Washington, Jackson firmly voted against it.

It was in Congress that Jackson first proved he could control his temper when it suited his interests. As a freshman congressman, he patiently worked his way through debates and committees to acquire legislation that was beneficial to the people of Tennessee.

In 1797 the Tennessee legislature elected him to the United States Senate. Congress now recognized him as "spokesman for the West," representing the characteristic of life in the newer regions of the United States — the rugged lands west of the Alleghenies. Although he fared well in the political arena, the intricacies of politics irked Jackson. He was involved in business troubles on his plantation back home that initiated his dislike of Eastern banks, especially the Bank of the

United States. He resented bank controls on loans. In the spring of 1798 he resigned from the Senate and was appointed judge of the supreme court, or superior court, of Tennessee. Although he lacked judicial experience, Jackson administered fair, unbiased justice.

CHAPTER 2

Military Feats

In 1802 Jackson was made a major general in the Tennessee militia. Jackson resigned from Tennessee's supreme court in 1804 and gave up political life. He devoted himself to paying off his personal debts, developing the Hermitage, and training the militia.

Jackson found himself in a precarious situation when he provided soldiers and boats to Aaron Burr under the impression that Burr was preparing to defend the Southwest against a Spanish attack. Jackson trusted Burr's intentions until he learned of President Jefferson's proclamation ordering the arrest of Burr and his cohorts. Burr was charged with attempting to form a secessionist movement to divide the Union and

Painting showing General Jackson astride his horse, leading the troops of the Tennessee militia. Library of Congress Prints and Photographs Division

was tried for treason in May 1807, but he was later acquitted. When these seditious plans unfolded, Jackson detached himself from any association with Burr.

THE WAR OF 1812

Soon came the turning point in Jackson's life—his spectacular service in the War of 1812. This was a conflict fought between the United States and Great Britain over British violations of U.S. maritime rights. To enforce its blockade of French ports during the Napoleonic Wars, the British boarded U.S. and other neutral ships to check cargo they suspected was being sent to France and to impress, or force into service, seamen alleged to be British navy deserters. The United States reacted by passing legislation such as the Embargo Act (1807) and the Non-Intercourse Act (1809), which placed restrictions on trade with Britain. Leaders in Congress also called for expulsion of the British from Canada to ensure frontier security. When the United States demanded an end to the interference, Britain refused, and the United States declared war on June 18, 1812.

Despite early U.S. naval victories, notably the duel between the *Constitution* and the

The U.S. Constitution (right) *destroying the British naval vessel the* Guerrière *during the early days of the War of 1812.* MPI/Archive Photos/Getty Images

Guerrière, Britain gradually established a firm blockade of eastern U.S. ports. A British force burned public buildings in Washington, D.C., including the White House, in 1814. The war became increasingly unpopular, especially in New England, where the war's interruption of commerce angered many.

CAMPAIGN AGAINST THE CREEK INDIANS

When the United States and Great Britain were on the brink of war, Jackson enlisted

Hand-drawn diagram indicating the position of American troops at Horseshoe Bend, where Jackson-led U.S. forces suppressed an uprising by Creek Indians in 1814. MPI/Archive Photos/Getty Images

nearly 50,000 volunteers into his militia. Once Congress had declared war on Great Britain, Jackson was ordered to suppress the Creek Indian uprisings in the South. Encouraged by the British attacks against the United States, the Creeks raided frontier settlements in Georgia and Alabama. After several ferocious skirmishes, Jackson and his Tennessee militia crushed the Creeks at the Battle of Horseshoe Bend, Ala., on March 27, 1814.

The Creek campaign was typical of Jackson as a man and as a general. He was not a great military strategist, but he had a strong determination to win. Without taking time to set up an adequate supply line, he relentlessly led his men through the winter wilderness in multiple attacks. Sometimes he and his men had only roasted acorns for food. He was sick throughout most of the campaign and his shoulder ached from a bullet wound sustained in a recent duel, but he never faltered. He quelled two mutinies that arose from lack of supplies and prevented a third by having a rebellious soldier shot. His troops considered him "tough as hickory," thus they nicknamed him Old Hickory. The decimated Creeks were forced to give up most of their rich lands in Georgia and Alabama. The triumph

General Jackson (on horseback) *putting a stop to one of several mutinies by U.S. troops facing hardships during the War of 1812.* **Library of Congress Prints and Photographs Division**

won acclaim for Jackson as a soldier, and he was commissioned as a major general in the U.S. Army.

THE BATTLE OF NEW ORLEANS

In November 1814 Jackson marched into Spanish-held Florida and captured Pensacola, preparing for the U.S. occupation of Florida. Prior to Jackson's arrival, the British army had evacuated the city and advanced by sea toward New Orleans. Consequently, Jackson

General Jackson shown leading the charge at the Battle of New Orleans. Although the battle had no impact on the outcome of the War of 1812, it was a defining moment in Jackson's life. **Library of Congress Prints and Photographs Division**

was ordered to organize a defense of New Orleans from an imminent British attack. He reached the city the following month, built fortifications, and established martial law.

To bolster his small regular army, Jackson recruited frontier riflemen from Tennessee and Kentucky and organized a force of volunteers—free blacks, planters, and pirates headed by Jean Lafitte. Beyond the crude U.S. ramparts of cotton bales lay experienced British troops who had fought in Europe's Napoleonic Wars. Beginning late in December 1814 the British bombarded the U.S. defenses, setting the cotton bale ramparts afire. Between skirmishes and British bombardments, Jackson's men tenaciously reinforced the city's fortifications with earthworks.

On Jan. 8, 1815, with only contempt for Jackson's amateur army, the British troops charged. The battle ensued as waves of British soldiers fell victim to the artillery of the U.S. defenders. Demoralized, the British withdrew after suffering more than 2,000 fatalities. Jackson sustained minimal casualties in what became known as the Battle of New Orleans.

The tragic mistake of the battle was that it was fought after the Treaty of Ghent was

Pirate and Patriot

The pirate Jean Lafitte was also a patriot. He interrupted his illicit adventures to fight heroically for the United States in defense of New Orleans in the War of 1812.

Little is known of Lafitte's early life, but by 1809 he and his brother Pierre had established in New Orleans a blacksmith shop that reportedly served as a depot for smuggled goods and slaves brought ashore by a band of privateers (sailors on private vessels licensed to attack enemy ships). Led by Lafitte, this group maintained an illegal colony on the secluded islands of Barataria Bay south of the city. Holding privateer commissions from the republic of Cartagena (in modern Colombia), Lafitte's group preyed mainly on Spanish ships. Because other business suffered from Lafitte's activities, he and his men were indicted as pirates. In 1814 his colony was destroyed by a United States Navy force. Lafitte managed to escape, however.

At this time the British offered Lafitte $30,000 for his allegiance in their planned attack on New Orleans. Instead, Lafitte warned Louisiana officials of the attack, but he was not believed. He then offered his aid to General Andrew Jackson, who accepted Lafitte's help in the ensuing Battle of New Orleans. During the battle Lafitte fought well. Later, President James Madison pardoned him and his men for their acts of piracy.

signed on Dec. 24, 1814, officially ending the war. News of the peace treaty did not reach Jackson in time to prevent the conflict. His victory in no way affected the outcome of the War of 1812, but it raised the morale of the country after the war ended in a stalemate. His superb military leadership in New Orleans earned him status as a national hero.

FIRST SEMINOLE WAR

President James Monroe ordered Jackson to the Alabama-Georgia region in December 1817 to defend U.S. settlers against attacks by the Seminoles from Florida and runaway slaves living among the tribes. In the spring of 1818, without awaiting further orders, Jackson marched into Spanish-held Florida and burned Seminole villages. He then captured Pensacola and St. Marks and hanged two British traders who were suspected of collaborating with the Seminoles. These actions, in what became known as the First Seminole War, threatened to involve the United States in war against both Great Britain and Spain. Monroe and Secretary of War John C. Calhoun felt that Jackson had exceeded his authority and should be

Statue of Andrew Jackson erected in Jacksonville, the Florida city named after the military hero. For a brief time Jackson was the military governor of Florida. © Kord.com/age fotostock/SuperStock

reprimanded, but Secretary of State John Quincy Adams argued that Jackson's exploits provided the United States with an opportunity to annex Florida from Spain.

When Spain ceded Florida to the United States in 1821, President Monroe appointed Jackson the military governor of the territory. Tiring of politics, Jackson resigned this post in late 1821 and retired to private life.

CHAPTER 3

Road to the Presidency

The United States was entering a new age of development as the presidential election of 1824 drew near. Foreign affairs were now of less concern than the internal improvements of the country. With the expansion of the West and the increase of small businesses and industries in the East, the changes in the nation called for a new voice to express the will of the "common people." The Western farmers and the Eastern laborers demanded a leader unbound by tradition. The diverse personalities of the candidates and sectional rivalries throughout the nation were the focal points of the election.

Political cartoon, published in 1824, depicting Jackson's opponents as snarling dogs. The presidential election of 1824 was rife with rivalries and conflict. Library of Congress Prints and Photographs Division

PRESIDENTIAL PROSPECTS

Jackson's military triumphs led to suggestions that he become a candidate for president, but he disavowed any interest, and political leaders in Washington assumed that the flurry of support for him would prove transitory. The campaign to make him president, however, was kept alive by his continued popularity and was carefully nurtured by a small group of his friends in Nashville, who combined devotion to the general with a high degree of political astuteness. In 1822 these friends maneuvered the Tennessee legislature into a formal nomination of their hero as a candidate for president. In the following year this same group persuaded the legislature to elect him to the U.S. Senate—a gesture designed to demonstrate the extent of his popularity in his home state.

THE ELECTION OF 1824 AND ITS AFTERMATH

The Tennessee legislature nominated the nontraditionalist Jackson for the presidency in 1824. He campaigned against Secretary of State John Quincy Adams of Massachusetts, Speaker of the House Henry Clay of Kentucky, and Treasury Secretary William H. Crawford of Georgia. The electoral results were: Jackson (99), Adams (84), Crawford

Portrait of Jackson highlighting his victory at the Battle of New Orleans. Jackson's supporters used his popularity as a war hero to gain him a presidential nomination. Library of Congress Prints and Photographs Division

(41), and Clay (37). Since none of the candidates received a majority, the Constitution required that the House of Representatives decide the outcome of the election.

Also, in accordance with the Twelfth Amendment to the Constitution, the House could choose from only the top three vote-getters. Subsequently, Clay was dropped from consideration, and he immediately endorsed Adams, who was thus elected the sixth president of the United States. When Adams named Clay his secretary of state, Jackson and his followers claimed that Adams and Clay had made a "corrupt bargain"—alleging that Clay supported Adams in exchange for a Cabinet appointment.

Enraged over his loss in the election, Jackson led a four-year chastisement of the Adams administration and referred to Clay as the "Judas of the West." Jackson resigned from the Senate in 1825, but his allies in Congress, the Jacksonians, set forth to undermine all of Adams' executive policies and decisions. The Jacksonians created the Democratic party and used Adams' term as a platform to promote Jackson for president in the election of 1828.

Cartoon imagining the top three vote-getters in the 1824 presidential election as participants in a foot race to the White House. Left to right, foreground: John Quincy Adams, William Crawford, Andrew Jackson. MPI/Archive Photos/Getty Images

THE ELECTION OF 1828

Jackson, the Democratic party candidate, swept the presidential election of 1828 by an electoral count of 178 to 83 cast for Adams as the National Republican. John C. Calhoun was reelected vice president. Jackson won a majority of his support from the South and West and, with the help of Senator Martin Van Buren of New York, carried the state of New York as well. Adams claimed the

Portrait of Henry Clay, who earned Jackson's distrust when he backed John Quincy Adams for president against Jackson in 1824. **Stock Montage/Archive Photos/Getty Images**

The support of Martin Van Buren, a senator from New York, was an important factor in Jackson winning the presidential election of 1828. Stock Montage/Archive Photos/Getty Images

New England states, but Jackson prevailed by securing overwhelming support from an enormous number of voters across the country.

Slanderous campaigning dominated the election. The Jacksonians, particularly the congressmen and landowners from Nashville, continuously criticized Adams for the "corrupt bargain" that he was accused of making in the election of 1824. In contrast, Jackson's political foes used the supposedly adulterous nature of his first

Breaking New Ground

The election of 1828 is commonly regarded as a turning point in the political history of the United States. Jackson was the first president from the area west of the Appalachians, but it was equally significant that the initiative in launching his candidacy and much of the leadership in the organization of his campaign also came from the West. The victory of Jackson indicated a westward movement of the center of political power. He was also the first man to be elected president through a direct appeal to the mass of the voters rather than through the support of a recognized political organization. Jackson once said: "I know what I am fit for. I can command a body of men in a rough way; but I am not fit to be president." Yet today he is regarded as the maker of the modern presidency.

marriage to Rachel in 1791 to defame his character and that of his wife. The details resurfaced about their first wedding before Rachel was legally divorced from her previous husband, and this news cast a negative shadow on Jackson's image. Rachel became overly distraught by the malignant propaganda circulating around the country, and on Dec. 22, 1828, she died of a heart attack. Jackson, devastated by the sudden loss of his wife, blamed her death on the treachery of his political opponents.

Satirical drawing of Andrew Jackson's first reception at the White House, from The Playfair Papers, *1841. Library of Congress, Washington, D.C.*

On March 4, 1829, the grief-stricken Jackson was inaugurated as the seventh president of the United States. The celebration of his inauguration riotously heralded a new era in U.S. politics. Hordes of people swarmed through the White House to cheer their hero, Old Hickory. The mass was so great that friends had to help the president escape through a side door.

CHAPTER 4

Presidency

When Jackson took office, many people in the East feared him. Thomas Jefferson earlier wrote, "I feel very much alarmed at the prospect of seeing General Jackson president. He is one of the most unfit men I know of for the place.... He is a dangerous man." Despite Jefferson's remarks, Jackson remained a strong advocate of the Jeffersonian principles of liberty and democracy.

Although inexperienced in public office compared to his predecessors, Jackson governed with the confidence of a strong-willed military commander. In policy-making, he relied on the notions of political allies such as Secretary of State Martin Van Buren and Secretary of War John H. Eaton. Instead of consulting other Cabinet members on

The Spoils System

Jackson's loyalty to his friends led him to expand what is known as the spoils system. This is the practice of discharging members of the defeated political party from public office and replacing them with members of the winning party. The system had been practiced previously in the federal government when Thomas Jefferson as president had removed Federalists for people in his own party. Jackson pledged to sweep the "corrupt" opposition out of office.

In answer to criticism of Jackson's policy on political appointments, Senator William L. Marcy of New York replied, "To the victor belong the spoils." Although Jackson was charged with abusing the spoils system, he in fact replaced less than 20 percent of current federal officeholders. The process of rewarding political service with public office helped to establish major political parties. In an effort to curb the excesses of the spoils system, Congress passed the Civil Service Act in 1883.

administrative decisions, Jackson conferred with an informal group of advisers that included newspaper editors Amos Kendall and Francis P. Blair, as well as Andrew Jackson Donelson, the president's nephew and personal secretary. Critics called these close friends of Jackson his "kitchen cabinet."

Statue of Francis Blair, which stands in the Hall of Columns in the U.S. Capitol. A close friend and advisor, Blair was a member of Jackson's "kitchen cabinet." Tom Williams/ CQ-Roll Call Group/Getty Images

CONFLICT OVER NULLIFICATION

The question of Jackson's successor became an issue soon after he assumed the presidency because of his poor health. Vice President Calhoun was a leading candidate, as was Secretary of State Van Buren. When news leaked in 1830 that Calhoun, as secretary of war during the Cabinet debates of 1818, had condemned Jackson's military actions in the First Seminole War, the president alienated Calhoun.

An intense rivalry developed between Jackson and Calhoun over a protective tariff and nullification. In 1828 President Adams had approved the Tariff of Abominations, a high tax on imported industrial goods to protect the New England factories from foreign competitors. Calhoun argued that the tariff oppressed the South and favored the Northern states. South Carolina, Calhoun's native state, was especially hostile toward the tariff and fought for the Southern states' right to nullify federal laws that were considered unconstitutional.

Although not an avid supporter of the tariff, Jackson reasoned that it was beneficial to trade relations with Europe and helped pay the national debt. At the same time, however, he despised nullification because he felt that it exceeded the limitations of states' rights, and tolerance of such a practice would destroy the Union.

To ease the tension with South Carolina, Jackson issued a reform tariff in 1832 that was less burdensome than the original. Not satisfied, South Carolina passed the Ordinance of Nullification that same year, thus declaring the tariff altogether null and void. South Carolina also threatened to secede from the Union if the federal government attempted to enforce the tariff within the state's boundaries. At the end of 1832, disgruntled with Jackson's policies, Calhoun resigned as vice president after South Carolina elected him to the U.S. Senate. Van Buren assumed the vice presidency in 1833.

The situation grew dire as Jackson readied U.S. armed forces in anticipation of an armed conflict with South Carolina. He threatened military intervention to collect the tariff duties if the state persisted in disregarding federal laws. The crisis was averted in 1833 when Senator Henry Clay of Kentucky proposed two compromise bills. The first bill reduced the tariff to an even more moderate level than the reform tariff of 1832. The second, named the Force Bill, authorized the president to use the military to enforce federal mandates in the states if necessary. South Carolina accepted the compromise bills and repealed its nullification act. Clay's shrewd negotiating skills successfully preserved the Union from a serious domestic threat.

CHALLENGES WITH NATIVE AMERICANS

Battles against the Creeks and Seminoles during his military career made Jackson unsympathetic toward Native Americans, and he sought to displace them from all areas east of the Mississippi River. Beginning in 1829 Georgia extended its territory into Cherokee lands that had been granted to them in a treaty with the U.S. government. Georgia desired these lands where gold had been discovered. Critics claimed that Georgia was infringing upon the rights of the Cherokees, but Jackson refused to interfere with Georgia's efforts. Instead, he signed the Indian Removal Act of 1830 that required all Native American tribes east of the Mississippi River to abandon

Painting by Robert Ottokar Lindneux depicting Native Americans of the Cherokee tribe marching to Oklahoma, a journey known as the Trail of Tears. © SuperStock

their homes and move to reservations provided by the U.S. government in the West.

The Cherokees appealed to the federal courts, and in 1832 the Supreme Court ruled that Georgia's actions were unconstitutional and declared that the state had no jurisdiction over Cherokee lands. Nevertheless, Georgia defied this decision and proceeded to encroach on Cherokee territory. Without Jackson's enforcement of the Supreme Court ruling, the Cherokees were evicted and forced to march west in the fall and winter of 1838–39. The frigid weather and lack of food supplies contributed to horrible suffering and so many deaths during this journey that the Cherokees named it the Trail of Tears.

The Indian Removal Act greatly angered many Native Americans, causing them to revolt. In 1831 a group of Sauk and Fox tribes led by Chief Black Hawk were forced to vacate their villages and fields along the Rock River in Illinois and move west of the Mississippi River into Iowa. The following year Black Hawk guided his people across the Mississippi River back into Illinois, provoking Governor John Reynolds to send an Illinois militia to fight the insurgent Native Americans. During the Black Hawk War of 1832, the Sauk and Fox tribes were slaughtered and Black Hawk was captured.

Another Native American tribe that defied Jackson's Indian policy was the

An artist's vision of Seminole Indians in Florida attacking a U.S. military fort during the Second Seminole War. **MPI/Archive Photos/ Getty Images**

Seminoles in Florida. Chief Osceola hid the tribal families in the Everglades and put up fierce resistance in the Second Seminole War that lasted from 1835 to 1842. Osceola's warriors resorted to guerrilla tactics in the fighting. It was a costly war that claimed nearly 2,000 U.S. casualties before Osceola was captured, and when a truce was called, most of the remaining Seminoles finally agreed to emigrate west. Jackson dealt harshly with the Native Americans whom he considered an obstacle to the expansion and growth of the nation.

ECONOMIC POLICIES

Internal improvements to the country were not a priority in Jackson's plan for economic stability. He believed that federally sponsored state projects were adverse to the welfare of the country because they led to regional disputes and promoted favoritism. When presented with the Maysville Road bill in 1830 that would have authorized federal funding for the 60-mile (100-kilometer) road in Kentucky stretching from Maysville to Lexington, Jackson quickly vetoed it. His concerns were for improvements advantageous to the entire nation, thus he approved the extension of the National Road, or Cumberland Road. More than any previous president, Jackson exercised the veto 12 times over the course of his administration.

As the "spokesman for the West," Jackson distrusted the powerful banks of the East. He especially detested the monopoly held by the Second Bank of the United States. With the bank's charter set to expire in 1836, Jackson's political opponents pushed the bill through Congress ahead of the presidential election of 1832 to challenge his stance on the measure.

He vetoed the new charter for the bank in July 1832, much to the delight of his admirers who also opposed the bank. He declared that its control of the nation's money was a menace both to private businesses and to the ideals of a democratic government.

Campaigning in the election of 1832 centered on the issue of the bank charter. This election marked the first time that presidential candidates were chosen at national party conventions. The National Republicans met in December 1831 in Baltimore, Md., and nominated Senator Henry Clay as their candidate

Political cartoon featuring President Jackson (second from right) *causing the downfall of the Second Bank of the United States. The bank's charter was a major issue during the election of 1832.* **Library of Congress Prints and Photographs Division**

to run against the incumbent Jackson, who was nominated for reelection in May 1832 at the Democratic National Convention also held in Baltimore. Martin Van Buren was Jackson's running mate for vice president. Clay's supporters attested that Jackson's veto of the bank charter impaired the financial security of the country.

Jackson's political adversaries considered him an enemy to states' rights because of his stance against nullification and because of his refusal to approve federal financing of internal improvements. His enemies referred to his administrative policies as executive tyranny and called him King Andrew I. The Whig party emerged in 1834 under the direction of Clay and was based on this anti-Jacksonian sentiment. Nevertheless, Jackson still carried the South and West in the election and prevailed with 219 electoral votes to only 49 for Clay.

The veto of the bank charter bill created controversy over financial policy in the United States that persisted throughout Jackson's second term. Although the bank's old charter still had three years to run, Jackson removed the government funds from it and deposited them in state banks, also referred to as his "pet" banks.

Jackson's Whig opponents are shown cutting down "Ol' Hickory" (Jackson's nickname) and ruining the national treasury "nest" at the top in this political cartoon. **Library of Congress Prints and Photographs Division**

The state banks were more lenient with the extension of credit, and they printed large quantities of paper money. An increase in western land speculation resulted, but with the federal bank dissolving, Jackson's challenge was to establish a sound U.S. currency. The inflationary circulation of bank notes contributed to credit abuses by creditors and speculators, and the value of the paper money became difficult to manage. Therefore, Jackson issued the Specie Circular in July 1836 that required payment in gold or silver coins for the sale of all public lands. Banks failed because they were unable to keep up with the demand for gold and silver, and the country was faced with soaring inflation.

LAST YEARS OF JACKSON'S ADMINISTRATION

Upholding stern principles made Jackson many enemies around the country. The first assassination attempt against a president occurred on Jan. 30, 1835, outside the U.S. Capitol. Richard Lawrence, a house painter, approached the president outside the Capitol and aimed a derringer in Jackson's

Image showing the attempted assassination of Jackson by Richard Lawrence. Jackson's policies were unpopular with some citizens, making him a target for political and even physical attacks. ©**Pantheon/ SuperStock**

direction. When Lawrence pulled the trigger, however, the gun misfired. Lawrence then pulled a second derringer and tried to shoot Jackson again, but this weapon also misfired. Lawrence was tried for the failed assassination and sentenced to a mental institution. Jackson, who was accustomed to gunplay from engaging in numerous duels, was spared once again.

Revolution in Texas erupted in December 1835 as settlers there fought the oppressive Mexican government that ruled the territory. The Alamo fell on March 6, 1836, as Mexican forces under Santa Anna stormed the fort in San Antonio after a 12-day siege and massacred every one of the defenders. The Texans fought the Mexican army aggressively until they finally prevailed. Texas won its independence from Mexico when Sam Houston, commander in chief of the Texan army, defeated and captured Santa Anna at San Jacinto. The Texans were encouraged in the battle by their war cry "Remember the Alamo!"

Jackson considered Texas vital to the security of the Southwest. He wanted to annex the territory for the United States but worried that sectional disputes could arise

Photograph of Sam Houston, the military leader who helped Texas gain independence from Mexico. Houston was elected president of the Republic of Texas, which Jackson declined to annex as a state. **MPI/Archive Photos/Getty Images**

over the issue of slavery when Texas applied for statehood. Therefore, he recognized Texas' independence and rejected annexation to avoid any conflicts within his party that might jeopardize Vice President Van Buren's candidacy for president.

Through his aggressive leadership and patronage, Jackson had welded together a new party—the Democratic party. He so controlled the party that he chose Van Buren as his successor. Van Buren won the election of 1836 and took office on March 4, 1837.

RETIREMENT

Jackson retired to the Hermitage after Van Buren's inauguration. The financial depression that began during Jackson's second term strained the market for his crops, and he was forced

The Hermitage as it stands in the present day. Upon leaving public life, Jackson retired to his mansion in Tennessee, although he still kept active as a political advisor. © age fotostock/SuperStock

to sell some of his land and borrow money to cover his farm expenses. He continued to advise his party leaders and to receive visitors at the Hermitage. From his home he stayed abreast of national politics and promoted Van Buren's unsuccessful run for reelection in 1840. Jackson rejoiced at the Democratic presidential nomination of fellow Tennessean James K. Polk in 1844 and supported the U.S. annexation of Texas in 1845.

Jackson's health had begun failing slowly throughout his presidency, and it gradually

Andrew Jackson's tomb, situated in a garden on the Hermitage grounds. KennStilger47/Shutterstock.com

worsened in his final years. He was stricken with tuberculosis and lost the eyesight in his right eye. Jackson died on June 8, 1845, in his home and was buried next to his wife in the Hermitage garden.

CONCLUSION

Jacksonian democracy represented the average U.S. citizen. Andrew Jackson was a man of the people, and his actions while in office found widespread approval and exercised a profound effect on the character of U.S. politics for half a century. The new Democratic party that developed in the 1830s was based on the former Jeffersonian principle of popular government. Old Hickory increased the power of the presidency through his hardhanded leadership and, at the same time, strengthened the nation by advocating policies that encompassed it as a whole.

Glossary

adverse Hard, difficult, or working against one's interests.

annexation The incorporation of a territory or nation into an existing nation or state.

aristocracy A privileged class of people who have considerable wealth and power.

charter A guarantee of rights and privileges given by the sovereign power of a state or country.

delirium A state of mind characterized by confusion, trouble communicating, and even seeing things that aren't there.

displace To force a person or group of people to move from their homeland.

encroach To move beyond the usual or stated limits.

infringe To illegally take possession of someone's physical or intellectual property.

land speculation Buying large areas of land at cheap prices and waiting to sell them later on once prices have risen.

militia A group of citizens organized for military service.

monopoly Having exclusive control of something.

nullification The action of a state impeding or attempting to prevent the operation and enforcement within its territory of a law of the United States.

orator A person with great public-speaking skills.

patronage The power to make appointments to government jobs, especially for political advantage.

precarious Of or related to being dependent on unknown or changing circumstances.

secessionist Activity related to the withdrawal of a state from a larger political body.

slander To speak out against someone in an attempt to do harm; especially lies and rumors.

squander To use something carelessly or wastefully, especially money.

tariff A tax on imported and exported goods and services.

truce When two sides of a conflict agree to stop fighting.

vacate To give up a position, willingly or by force.

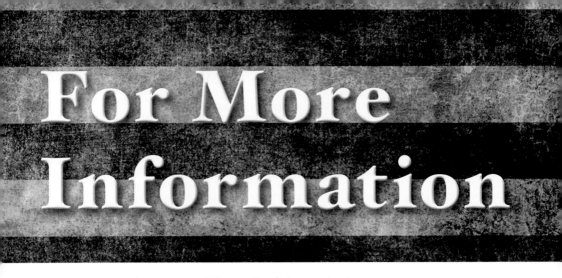

For More Information

American Historical Association
400 A Street SE
Washington, DC 20003
(202) 544-2422
Web site: http://www.historians.org
The American Historical Association is a
professional organization for historians,
researchers, and students. The association also offers important resources and
publications for anyone interested in the
history of the United States.

Andrew Jackson State Park
196 Andrew Jackson Park Road
Lancaster, SC 29720
(803) 285-3344
Web site: http://www.southcarolinaparks
.com/andrewjackson
Andrew Jackson State Park honors the seventh president of the United States with
events celebrating the life and times
of Andrew Jackson. The park includes

a living history program that details Jackson's boyhood and chronicles life in the area during the late 18th century.

The Hermitage
4580 Rachel's Lane
Nashville, TN 37076
(615) 889-2941
Web site: http://www.thehermitage.com
Visitors to the Hermitage can tour Andrew Jackson's historic home and grounds and learn all about his life and presidency through featured exhibits at the Andrew Jackson Visitor Center Gallery.

Miller Center
2201 Old Ivy Road
Charlottesville, VA 22904
(434) 924-7236
Web site: http://millercenter.org
The Miller Center at the University of Virginia furthers understanding of all aspects of the U.S. presidency, political history, and policy through various research initiatives, programs, events, and fellowship opportunities.

National Museum of American History
14th Street and Constitution Avenue NW
Washington, DC 20002
(202) 633-1000

Web site: http://americanhistory.si.edu

With more than 3 million artifacts of American history in its collection, the National Museum of American History is dedicated to promoting public interest in the events that shaped the American nation. Its "The American Presidency: A Glorious Burden" exhibit profiles American presidents through collections of their belongings.

Organization of American Historians
112 North Bryan Avenue
Bloomington, IN 47408
(812) 855-7311
Web site: http://www.oah.org

The Organization of American Historians is committed to advancing scholarship in the field of American history through programs, publications, and resources for students, teachers, researchers, and professionals in the field.

WEB SITES

Due to the changing nature of Internet links, Rosen Educational Services has developed an online list of Web sites related to the subject of this book. This site is updated regularly. Please use this link to access the list:

www.rosenlinks.com/pppl/anjack

For Further Reading

Buchanan, John. *Jackson's Way: Andrew Jackson and the People of the Western Waters* (Wiley, 2001).

Collier, Christopher, and Collier, James Lincoln. *Andrew Jackson's America, 1824–1850* (Benchmark Books, 1999).

Harmon, Daniel E. *Andrew Jackson* (Mason Crest Publishers, 2003).

Marrin, Albert. *Old Hickory: Andrew Jackson and the American People* (Dutton Children's Books, 2004).

Meacham, Jon. *American Lion: Andrew Jackson in the White House* (Random House, 2008).

Reynolds, David S. *Waking Giant: America in the Age of Jackson* (Harper, 2008).

Somervill, Barbara A. *Andrew Jackson* (Compass Point Books, 2003).

Stefoff, Rebecca. *The War of 1812* (Benchmark Books, 2001).

Whitelaw, Nancy. *Andrew Jackson: Frontier President* (Morgan Reynolds, 2001).

Wilentz, Sean. *Andrew Jackson* (Times Books, 2005).

Index